The Young Golfer

Vivien Saunders
and Clive Cl

Stanley Paul

London Melbourne Sydney Auckland Johannesburg

Also by Vivien Saunders
The Complete Woman Golfer
The Golfing Mind

Photographs by Peter Dazeley
and Bob Drummond

Stanley Paul & Co Ltd
An imprint of Century Hutchinson Ltd

62–65 Chandos Place, London, WC2N 4NW

Century Hutchinson Publishing (Australia) Pty Ltd
16–22 Church Street, Hawthorn
Melbourne, Victoria 3122

Century Hutchinson (NZ) Ltd
32–34 View Road, PO Box 40–086
Glenfield, Auckland 10

Century Hutchinson (SA) Pty Ltd
PO Box 337, Bergvlei 2012, South Africa

First published 1977
Reprinted 1980, 1984, 1986
© Vivien Saunders and Clive Clark 1977

Set in Monotype Times and Univers

Printed and bound in Great Britain by
Anchor Brendon Ltd, Tiptree, Essex

ISBN 0 09 131731 2

Contents

	Introduction	4
1	The Grip	5
2	The Stance	15
3	A Swing for Beginners	19
4	Perfecting the Backswing	24
5	Perfecting the Throughswing	28
6	Iron Shots	34
7	Fairway Woods	37
8	Using the Driver	38
9	Common Faults	42
10	Sloping Lies	46
11	Chipping	50
12	Pitching	55
13	Putting	60
14	Bunker Shots	67
15	Learning from Others	73
16	Becoming a Champion	84
17	Equipment	94
18	Par and Handicapping	102
19	Scoring in Golf	105
20	Etiquette	110
	Golfing Terms	112

Introduction

Why a golf book written for juniors? The needs of the junior golfer are often very different from those of the adult. Most adults find the golf swing difficult; the junior, on the other hand, will usually find the swing comparatively easy and learn very largely by imitation rather than from instructions. For this reason, the book is centred around eight action strips of the authors, which will give the young golfer a pattern on which to model himself – not just for the basic swing, but also in the various other shots which the successful player needs.

Instruction is given on every aspect of golf – right from learning as a beginner to playing in junior tournaments. The level of instruction ranges from simple ideas for the really young junior to ideas on practice and theory for the teenager aspiring to top-class golf. In addition, there are some guides for the golfing parent on the best way to help a young player with his golf.

1. The Grip

For the junior golfer, the grip is almost certainly the most important part of the game. Unfortunately, it is also the most difficult. The way you grip the club controls the height, direction and distance of the shots you can produce.

The main aim of the golf grip is to set the right hand in a strong hitting position behind the club. The right hand has to face out along the hole to the target, with the power in the hand aimed where you are trying to hit the ball. In this way, the right hand produces a powerful hit and also helps strike the ball in the right direction. So we are aiming at setting the right hand *behind* the club to give power and direction to the shot.

The left hand

Firstly, in gripping the club, sit the clubhead flat on the ground with the bottom of the club aimed at your target. This is called a square clubface. If you don't do this, you won't hit the ball straight. Now take hold of the club with the left hand – half an inch or so from the top of the club. Bring the left hand into a position so that the tip of the thumb and first finger are close together, forming a line or 'V' between

Sequence A
Vivien Saunders – a full
6-iron shot

Sequence B
The 6-iron from behind

Sequence C
Clive Clark demonstrates a
powerful drive

Sequence D
The drive from behind

5

the two. This line or 'V' should seem to point up to your right ear or right shoulder. You should now see two or three knuckles of this hand, but never the fourth. Lastly, see that the tip of the thumb and first joint of the index finger are more or less level – not with the thumb stretched down the club (Photo 1).

The right hand – Vardon grip

From here, let's look at how the right hand is added to the grip. In fact there are three ways of doing this. The first is the Vardon grip – made popular by Harry Vardon who was the world's outstanding golfer at the beginning of this century. This is the most common of the three grips and the best to learn if your hands are large enough.

The first stage in learning this is to separate the little finger of the right hand from the other three. Rest the club diagonally across these three fingers, with the little finger of the right hand hanging out behind (Photo 2). Now bring the right hand up so that you fit the fold at the bottom of the right palm against the base of the left thumb. Fold the right hand over

1/2/3 Forming the basic grip. Turn the book upside down to see how the grip will look to you. The important keys are the lines between thumb and first finger of both hands, pointing up to your right ear or shoulder.

6

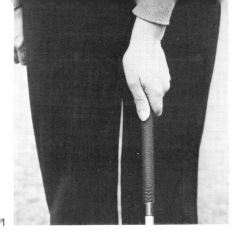

Points to watch in this action are the steady position of the head, the freedom of movement in the legs and the relative lengths of backswing and throughswing

At the top of the backswing the club points along the line of the shot and then swings right through and over the left shoulder in the followthrough. Notice the whole direction of the swing

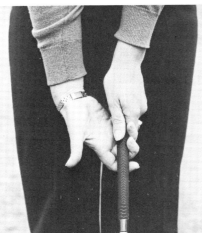

The main point to watch in the drive is the way in which the head is always well behind the ball as you strike it – the back arching and the legs moving fast and freely in the throughswing

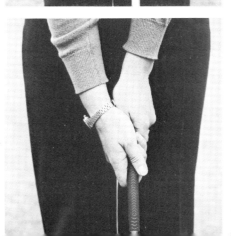

The club points straight out along the fairway at the top of the backswing, shoulders turned. The head is kept perfectly still during the whole swing and yet arms and legs are moving really fast

4   The overlapping, Vardon grip.

and the two should feel as though they were really made to fit together if you do this correctly. The left thumb should now be covered as well as possible (Photo 3). Again you should see a line or 'V' between the thumb and first finger, pointing up to the same spot as the 'V' in the left hand – in other words to about the right ear. Having done this, try to wrap the little finger of the right hand around the joint of the first finger of the left (Photo 4). This is only possible if your fingers are long enough and the grips of your club thin enough. Look down at the grip and check that the tip of the right thumb and joint of the first finger are more or less level, just as they were in the left hand.

The interlocking grip

For those of you starting as really young juniors or with rather small

8

5   Jack Nicklaus's interlocking grip.

hands, the Vardon grip is probably going to seem difficult. The little finger may simply not be long enough to fit around the outside of the other hand. For you, a better alternative is the interlocking grip, which is the one used by Jack Nicklaus (Photo 5). The club is gripped as before, but with the little finger of the right hand and index finger of the left hooked together – both fingertips outwards. The hands are now joined firmly and may fit together more easily.

The baseball grip

The last alternative is the baseball grip – just a simple two-handed grip with all eight fingers on the club. This is really the grip for only the youngest of juniors to try, when their hands are so small that the other two grips are both impossible. A number of very good players have used this grip, but unless

9

you are very careful, your hands can slip apart with this one. As soon as your hands are large enough, change to one of the other two grips. They are really much better.

Grip tension

Many golfers hold the club too tightly. The fault with this is that it stops the hands and wrists working fast and freely in the downswing. This produces loss of distance. The grip pressure should be rather like that in holding a small animal or bird – firm enough so as not to let go, of course, but not too tight.

What does the grip do?

The important point about the grip is that it controls the face of the club – the part which hits the ball. The grip is extremely important because it is your only contact with the club.

To hit the ball straight, the clubface must look at the target and not to either right or left. We start with it there as we grip the club and must bring it back there as we strike the ball. This is where the grip – in particular the right hand – is important. What you should feel is that the right hand is always very much *behind* the club so that it is aimed at the flag. It can then work in partnership with the clubface. As

10

your right hand travels down and through in the swing, the palm of the hand will usually face the target, as though slapping the ball in the right direction. This will bring the clubface to the ball aimed correctly.

The incorrect grip

What most of you will do – almost every junior golfer does – is to put the right hand very much *under* the club in the grip. This will probably feel strong and more comfortable than the correct grip and probably give you the feeling of being able to lift the ball into the air. Now as you look down at the grip, you will see all the fingernails of the right hand, and the line or 'V' between the thumb and first finger will point way outside the right shoulder. This is very wrong (Photo 6).

What happens with this grip is that during the swing, the right hand will be turned to face the target, twisting the club so that it looks to the left (Photo 7). This 'closed' position of the clubface sends the ball curving away to the left – the hook – also producing a shot which is much too low. So, always remember in the grip, that the right hand must face down the fairway to your target, the club resting in the fingers, so that the strength in the right hand is behind – *not under* – the club.

11

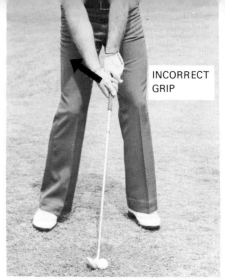

6/7 If the right hand is too far under the club at address it tends to close the clubface at impact, producing low shots to the left.

Ideas for practice

For a good golfer, the grip should always be exactly the same at the end of the swing as it was at the beginning. The grip should never loosen or change in any way. A good exercise, once you have developed your basic swing, is to try to hit one shot after another without the hands moving. Start with a row of four balls in front of you. Hit the first ball. Try to keep the hands firm on the club and move forward to the second ball. Hit this. Again, keep the hands firm and move forward to the third ball. Hit this, and so on with the fourth. If you can learn to hit three or four balls away without changing the position of the

IMPACT

7

hands, you will begin to develop a firm, powerful grip (Photo 8).

A word for parents

Unless you are a good golfer yourself, you probably won't fully appreciate the importance of a good grip. But it is the basis of your junior's swing. If he has a bad grip, he will only start swinging poorly to counteract this.

The following five points should be remembered:

1 Ensure that the grips on your junior's clubs are thin enough and in good condition. A slippery grip will cause the hands to grip too tightly.

2 Stress the idea of the right hand being aimed on-target and not under the club.

13

8   Hitting a row of four balls without any movement in the hands will help produce a good grip.

3   Check that the 'V's in both hands always point just inside the right shoulder.

4   See that your junior has plenty of professional help with the grip. It is usually the most unnatural and difficult part of the game for a youngster to learn, so don't let him be discouraged by the awkward feel of the correct grip. This uncomfortable feeling will quickly pass.

5   Gripping too tightly will stifle the speed of the clubhead and lead to loss of distance and feel.

2. The Stance

There are two main points about the stance – also called the 'set-up' or 'address' position. Firstly, the stance prepares the body, arms and legs to move correctly. It has to be an active 'ready' position – knees relaxed – like waiting to receive service at tennis, or facing the bowler in cricket. Secondly, the stance must aim the body and swing in the right direction.

Front view

Let's look first at the way the set-up prepares us for the swing. First learn this with one of the medium irons – the 5, 6 or 7. Sit the clubhead flat on the ground, aimed at the target and with the correct grip. At this stage, stand opposite the ball with the feet together. Now spread them apart, each moving about six inches to the side so that the feet are about the width of your shoulders, with the ball opposite the middle of the stance. Just turn the feet out slightly – the left perhaps a little more than the right – and keep the weight rather on the insides of the feet with the knees knocked inwards just a little (Photo 9).

Now for the arms and hands. The hands should always be level or slightly ahead of the ball – never behind it. Just

15

9   Tom Weiskopf. The basic iron stance.

10   *Opposite*: Hale Irwin. Notice the direction of the feet, knees and shoulders, all parallel to the line of the shot.

let the arms hang loosely at address – the left fairly straight but not stiff. When you grip the club, the right hand is below the left. This means that the right shoulder will be pulled down slightly below the left shoulder. Just let this happen naturally and also relax the right arm slightly so that the right elbow seems a little tucked in. This will help your arms work correctly in the swing. Remember, one of the main aims of the stance is to make it as easy as possible to swing correctly.

16

Side view

From this view, it is clear that there is a slight angle between the arms and the club (Photo 10). This helps give the right type of position in the backswing. The hands aren't up at their highest but are dropped four or five inches. Here you can also see the right type of posture – not just a slouching or drooping from the shoulders – but with the bottom sticking out a little and the knees just slightly bent.

The other main point in the set-up is aiming. What you should feel in aiming the shot is that you are hitting along a pair of parallel lines – like railway lines. The ball is to be aimed down the right-

17

hand line with your body lined up down the left-hand one. This means that the lines across the toes, knees, hips and shoulders point down the fairway in the direction you want to hit the ball.

Of these four, it is the shoulders which are by far the most important. They are also the hardest to get right – both for amateurs and professionals. Remember that the right hand is below the left and so pulls the right shoulder down slightly. What can also happen is that the right shoulder gets pulled forward instead of down. This means that the shoulders are aimed to the left of target – a very bad fault in the set-up which produces a poor swing.

Distance

How far do you stand from the ball? This is clearly going to vary from one club to another. With the woods you are going to stand much further from the ball than with the short irons. A good guide is to keep the right elbow fairly close to the body at address – perhaps three or four inches away. If you move much further away than this, the set-up may feel very powerful but you will find the direction of your shots is poor. So get the right amount of bend in the body, sticking the bottom out a little, but don't push the arms out too far away from the side.

3. A Swing for Beginners

Whenever you are learning something new in the swing or correcting a fault, do as the professionals do, and practise with one of the medium irons – the 5, 6 or 7. *Don't* start with a wood or long iron.

Let's look at what we are really doing in the golf swing. Flick through the action strips and you will see what the golf swing should look like. From the address position, the body simply turns to the right and the arms are lifted. From there, the body turns through to the left and the arms swing down and up to the other side. This is the simple golf swing and the one you must learn first. And don't try to swing too hard at this stage!

The simple backswing

To learn this, start with the correct stance and grip. Feel at this point that the tip of the left thumb is roughly on the top of the club. This is important because the left thumb is going to guide the hands and arms in the swing. Now feel that you turn the body a little to the right – allowing the left heel to pull off the ground – and at the same time lift the arms. Bend the wrists slightly as you do this. This is where the left thumb

19

11   The simple backswing – club supported on the left thumb.

is important. You should now feel that the left thumb is supporting the club at the top of your swing (Photo 11).

The throughswing

From the top of the backswing, your body has to turn through to face your imaginary target while the arms swing down and up to the other side. Simply feel that your left heel pushes back down again, turning through so that you are balanced on the left foot and the tips of the toes of the right foot. Swish the club down and lift the arms to the left – just the opposite of what you did in the

20

12 The basic throughswing – facing your imaginary target. Notice the footwork.

backswing (Photo 12). Once again, the club should be supported on the left thumb – very important. Both arms will be slightly bent and, if you are turned to your imaginary target, the right arm will seem rather in front of your face. Again, check that you are balanced on the tips of the toes of the right foot.

Those are the three basic positions in the simple swing: the address, the backswing and the throughswing.

Learning to hit the ball

The thing to remember when you first start golf is that the golf ball is very

small. Because of this, you will only hit it well if the swing is exactly right. It is important to practise over and over again without the ball before expecting to hit it well. You will always see professionals practising their swing without the ball – often before every shot – so that practice swings are where you can often learn most. Therefore, practise your swing over and over again. Turn to the right and swing the arms up. Turn through to the left and swing the arms up. Check that at each end of the swing the club is supported on the left thumb. In the throughswing, make sure you are balanced on the left foot and the tips of the toes of the right.

As you practise this, swish the club through, brushing the ground at the spot where the ball would be. Only when you can brush the ground in the right place ten times out of ten should you try this with the ball. If you can't brush the ground correctly, you won't hit the ball well. Now try this with the ball. First start with the ball sitting up on a little tuft of grass. If you can brush the little tuft away, the ball will fly into the air. If you don't brush the tuft away, the ball will probably simply run along the ground. If you have real difficulty with this, practise with the ball on a low tee-peg, sweeping the peg away on each shot. One last thing – the clubhead has to strike the *back* of the ball, so fix

22

your eyes on the back of the ball and *not* the top of it, then simply repeat your swing. Turn and lift the arms. Turn through and lift the arms and concentrate on watching the back of the ball and brushing away the tuft of grass.

Don't try to hit the ball too hard at first. Just brush the grass and then turn through and check the balance in the throughswing. Right from the start, make the end of the swing look balanced and controlled. Have lots and lots of practice swings, brushing the grass exactly where you want.

Nick Faldo at practice.

23

4. Perfecting the Backswing

We will now assume you have learnt the basic swing and can brush the ground quite well and send the ball flying. Golf is a very exact game so you will need to develop the swing further to control your shots accurately. Let's look at the backswing in more depth. This can best be seen by studying action sequences A to D.

The arms

The left arm is really the key to a good backswing. It should start by hanging straight at address and then swing across your chest towards the right shoulder, shoulders turning, so that the arm stays straight. The left thumb should support the club at the top of the backswing. In fact, the left arm is so important in the backswing, that you should really feel that this does all the work in taking the club back.

The right arm starts in a more relaxed position at address and bends or folds in the backswing so that it forms a right angle – like the corner of a square – at the top of the swing. The elbow should point straight downwards, with the right hand almost beneath the club (Photo 13).

13 Johnny Miller. A really wound up backswing – club on-target, shoulders turned and left heel eased off the ground.

In a perfect backswing, the club should point exactly along the line of the shot – in other words, along the left-hand railway line we saw in the set-up.

The legs

Many people think because golf is a game where there is no running about, that the legs aren't important. But they are. Good professionals often train as hard with their legs as do runners and footballers because they are so important. A lot of power in the golf swing comes from the legs, so that they must move into the right position in the backswing.

In the basic beginner's swing, the body simply turns and the left heel pulls off the ground. As you develop your backswing, make certain that the left knee points at or behind the ball as you reach the top (Photo 13). With some players, this pulls the left heel off the ground. With others, the left heel stays down. Always give the heel freedom to come up if it wants to. If you try to keep it flat on the ground, it may stop you turning well in the backswing. If you look at the right leg, it must always stay slightly bent in the backswing – never allow the right leg to straighten back.

Practising the backswing

If you want to be a good golfer, keep practising the backswing. If you can do this in front of a mirror, all the better. Feel that all the movement is in the left side. Swing the club back with the *left* arm. Support the club on the *left* thumb. Point the *left* knee in at the ball and think of turning the *left* shoulder and not the right. Always check, too, that the club points in the right direction as this will control whether you hit the ball at the target or not. Lastly, if you haven't got room to swing a club in front of a mirror, you can practise the actions quite simply without a club. Form your ordinary grip, but hook the fingers together as in the interlocking grip, and this will keep your hands together well enough to practise the arm and leg movements in a limited space.

Tom Watson in action.

27

5. Perfecting the Throughswing

14

15

14/15/16/17 Johnny Miller. A perfect down and throughswing. Look at the enormous pull backwards with the left leg, right foot spinning onto the tips of the toes in the followthrough. The head is perfectly still long after the ball has gone.

16

17

The leg action

The leg action in the throughswing provides much of the power in the swing. At the top of the backswing, the left knee is pointing in towards the ball, with the left heel probably pulled slightly off the ground (Photo 14). In the throughswing there are three important stages to the leg action:

1 Push the left heel firmly down to the ground and keep it there through the rest of the swing (Photo 15).

2 Straighten the left leg as you start the swing down and twist the leg so that it remains straight with the left knee almost facing the target in your finish position (Photo 16).

3 Let the right knee kick through with the downswing so that you spin onto the tips of the toes of the right foot (Photo 17).

If your legs work correctly, at the end of the throughswing, you should be perfectly balanced on the left foot with the left leg straight, and on the toes of the right foot. This allows your whole body to finish facing the target as it should. The most common incorrect leg action is for the left leg to stay bent in the followthrough – the knee bending to the target (Photo 18). If this happens, try hard to pull the knee straight as you swing through, twisting the leg – not bending it.

30

18 Incorrect legwork. The left leg is buckling outwards. Compare this with photo 16 (page 29).

The arm action

The start of the downswing has to be done very much with the left arm. Feel as though you are pulling down hard with the left hand – not starting with the right. This will give you a correct 'late hit' position which is seen in every good golfer (Photo 15). From here, the right hand can hit as hard and fast as possible without spoiling the direction of the shot.

What is important is that the arms and hands move into the correct positions after hitting the ball and at the end of the swing. If they are correct

at the top of the backswing and correct again in the followthrough, they will almost certainly be right as you hit the ball. Just beyond impact, there is a moment when both arms should be straight, though not stiff. From there, the left arm must be allowed to fold into the body, just as the right one did in the backswing. At the end of the swing, both arms should therefore be bent, the left more than the right. The left thumb supports the club and the club will be pointing straight back over the left shoulder (Photo 17).

One last point to check. See that the right arm is up in front of the chin in the followthrough, and partly in front of the face. This will mean your swing has been aimed correctly on-target.

The important followthrough

Many golfers think that the finish of the swing is unimportant. They will usually say, 'How can anything I do after hitting the ball affect my shot?'

This idea is quite wrong. A good followthrough must be the aim of your swing, for if you swing from the correct backswing to a good finish, the swing through the ball will be right. There are three important things to check in the followthrough:

1 Are your legs in the right position – are you on the toes of your right foot with your left leg straight?

32

2 Is your grip just as firm as when you started?

3 Are you perfectly balanced?

Practising the throughswing

In every shot you hit – in practice and on the course – try to hold a firm followthrough for a definite count of 1, 2, 3. If you can do this, it helps you check the rest of the swing, keeps you balanced and stops you from trying to hit too hard. Learn to get in the same followthrough position on every full shot – balanced for the count of 3.

A word for parents

Stress the importance of the follow-through as much as possible – holding it for the count of 3. Ensure that there is perfect balance on the left foot and toes of the right, that the hips are turned through to face the target and that the left leg is firm. Almost every great golfer has a perfectly poised finish. Stress this to your junior.

33

6. Iron Shots

The basic swing you have learnt is really the same for all the clubs – woods and irons. The way you strike the ball is just slightly different.

With an iron shot, there are two basic ways of hitting the ball. These vary with the lie of the ball – in other words the amount of grass it sits on. In a good 'lie', the ball sits up on a little grass. In a bad or 'tight' lie, the ball sits down without any cushion of grass beneath it. Usually you will find shots from a good lie rather easier than from a bad lie.

When the lie is good, the ball can simply be brushed away, clipping the little piece of grass on which it sits. To do this, the ball is positioned just ahead of the centre of your stance – slightly nearer the left foot than the right. Just watch the back of the ball and sweep it away.

Taking a divot

When the lie is bad or tight, you can't just sweep the ball away as before. This time you need to hit the ball while the club is still travelling downwards – almost as though you are trying to dig the ball out. The ball is now played in the centre of the stance or even slightly towards the right foot. With these shots, one has to concentrate on pushing hard

34

19   Jack Nicklaus taking a divot with a short iron.

down onto the left heel in the through-swing and on trying to strike the ball and then take a little grass beyond this – a divot (Photo 19).

The short irons should always be played like this, taking a divot whether the lie is good or bad. With the long and medium irons, it is best to sweep the ball away from a good lie, only taking a divot when the lie is bad.

35

Timing

Remember with iron shots that the clubs will naturally produce different distance shots, provided you keep the swing exactly the same. Many golfers feel they have to swing much harder with the 3 and 4-irons to make the ball go further. In doing this, they rush the swing and ruin the shot. Keep the swing the same with every club. If you practise most with a 5, 6 or 7-iron, swing the long irons at exactly the same speed and in the same way. The design of the clubs gives you the different length and height of shot.

Severiano Ballesteros – a powerful iron shot

7. Fairway Woods

Wood shots from the fairway are played in much the same way as iron shots. First of all, look at how the ball is lying. Is it sitting nicely on a little grass, or sitting right down on a bare piece of ground? The way in which the ball is sitting is going to tell you which type of contact you want with the ball.

The good lie

If the ball sits nicely on some grass, you will simply sweep the ball away, brushing the little piece of grass on which it sits. The ball will now be positioned a little ahead of the centre of your stance – in other words slightly towards the left foot. Remember to watch the back of the ball and just think of sweeping it away.

The bad lie

When there is no grass between the ball and the ground, the shot is a little more difficult. As with an iron shot from this type of lie, you will almost have to hit the ball with the club still travelling downwards – in other words, squeezing the ball out. As with an iron shot from a bad lie, play the ball a little further towards the right foot or right from the middle of the stance. A good tip is to keep the hands slightly ahead of the ball – feeling that you hit the ball downwards, taking a little grass beyond.

37

8. Using the Driver

Driving is a very important part of golf. If you can drive well, it sets you up for the next shot along the fairway or onto the green. If you are always in the rough from the tee, it makes scoring very difficult.

Teeing the ball

If you compare a driver with one of the fairway woods, you will see that it is much deeper in the face. This is so that you can tee the ball up three-quarters of an inch or so, strike it well and get maximum distance. The way in which you tee the ball is important. If you can tee it the same height everytime, it helps you to produce the same shot. To tee the ball, hold it on top of the tee and push the tee into the ground with the ball. It should then balance first time. *Don't* simply try to stick the tee into the ground and then perch the ball on top of it. As you push the tee into the ground, try to judge the height. It will probably be a little more than the thickness of your fingers. When the ball is teed correctly, the centre of the ball should be just about the same height as the top of the head of your driver. If you drive with a 2 or 3-wood, the tee will have to be slightly lower. Adjust the height so that the top of the

20 The drive is the only shot where the ball is struck on the upswing. Notice the correct tee height.

wood is level with the centre of the ball (Photo 20).

The ball position

The swing is much the same for the driver as the other clubs, but the ball is contacted in a completely different way. This is the only shot in golf where the ball is hit with the club travelling upwards (Photo 20). This is purely because it can be teed up. To do this, it is important to position the ball ahead of the centre of the stance – almost opposite the left heel. Your swing will

39

21 The body should stay very much *behind* the ball with the drive, legs working hard.

now be much the same as with the other clubs. Brush the ground opposite the middle of the stance but collect the ball as the club starts its upswing (Photo 21).

Practising driving

In order to strike the ball correctly with the driver, you will need to do lots of practice swings. Choose a spot on the ground opposite your left heel where the ball would be. Look at this spot; but in the practice swing, make sure that the club brushes the ground three or four inches behind it. This means that you would now be able to strike the ball correctly on the upswing.

With the driver, position the ball opposite the left heel and concentrate on sweeping the ball away on the upswing. Many players like to feel that they make a wider, more stretched backswing with the driver than the other shots. Whether you feel this or not, work on good balance in the followthrough. This will stop you from trying to hit *too* hard. Hold the followthrough for a count of 1, 2, 3. If you can, you will probably hit a good drive. If you can't, work on balance – not distance.

41

9. Common Faults

The topped shot

This is when the ball just runs along the ground, without lofting into the air. The problem here is that the club strikes the ball somewhere round its middle instead of right at the bottom. If this is your problem, firstly check that you are looking at the back of the ball – the part you are going to hit – and not straight down on the top of the ball. If you still top the ball, concentrate on brushing the grass over and over again in practice swings. The chances are that you are trying to help the ball up into the air and so swinging the club upwards. All you need to do to get a ball to fly into the air is to swing the club *down* so that you brush the ground. The angle of the clubface will make the ball rise.

Low or hooked shots

If you strike the ball solidly but instead of flying high and straight, it travels off low, hooking away to the left, look at your grip. If your right hand gets too much *under* the club so that the 'V' between the thumb and index finger points way outside your right shoulder, this is the shot you are likely to produce (Photos 6 & 7). Remember the most basic rule in the grip is to keep the club

42

resting in the fingers of the right hand with the palm aimed powerfully down the fairway to your target. If the right hand starts under the club, it will twist it in the downswing and produce these low shots to the left. So forget whether the grip feels comfortable or not, and concentrate on aiming the right hand at the target from *behind* the club.

The slice

If you slice the ball – in other words, if it curves out to the right – you are probably not using your hands correctly in the swing. As you strike the ball, your hands should almost feel as if they are throwing the clubhead through the ball. If you don't get this throwing action with the hands, the clubface will be aimed to the right as the ball is struck and the ball will curve away to the right.

Again, check that the right hand is *behind* the club at address – not either under or on top of it – and feel that the wrists are a little looser as you swish through the ball. Think of the swish of the club and this should help you use your hands more correctly. One word of warning. If you use clubs which are too heavy or stiff, you are very likely to produce this shot. If this could be the problem, ask the advice of your club professional.

43

22 Incorrect. A downward contact with the driver produces high, skied shots.

High drives

Many golfers are troubled by skied drives – shots with the driver which seem to go almost straight up into the air, losing lots of distance. The first thing to look at in this case is the height of the tee. If the centre of the ball is higher than the top of your wood, you can quite simply go under the ball.

If the height of the tee is right, it means that you are almost certainly not getting the correct upward contact on the ball that you should. Remember that the ball has to be struck on the upswing with the drive. If you hit downwards at the ball like a short iron shot, you are quite likely to catch the ball from the top of the clubhead – leaving paint marks on the top of your wood (Photo 22). To correct this, make certain that the ball is played from opposite the left heel or just inside it, and think always of sweeping the ball away on the upswing. In your practice swing, try to brush the ground three or four inches behind the spot where the ball would be, so that the club is travelling upwards as the ball is hit. Hit upwards and the ball will go lower.

A word for parents

The main source of problems for the young golfer is in the grip. Really do ensure that both lines between the thumb and index finger point parallel to one another and somewhere between the chin and right shoulder. The worst fault is when the right hand slips under the club. This initially produces low shots hooked to the left. Ultimately, however, your junior will develop a bad swing to compensate for a bad grip and this will lead to considerably more problems at a later stage. The other main checkpoints are that the club aims along the desired line of flight in the backswing and that the weight is transferred onto the left heel and tips of the toes of the right foot in the follow-through.

45

10. Sloping Lies

Standing above the ball

When you have to stand above the ball, you will need to bend over more, producing a higher backswing. This tends to make the ball slice away to the right. Simply allow for this by aiming the whole of your shot well to the left of your target (Photo 23). Remember that the ball is likely to land on ground which also slopes this way and so will kick even further to the right. As far as the swing goes, the main point is to

23 Standing above the ball, the shot fades out to the right.

ensure that you really stay down as you strike it, watching the ball just as long as you can. So aim left and stay down.

Standing below the ball

Standing below the ball produces just the opposite effect. You will be pushed further from the ball and this means the body bends less, taking the swing flatter round the body. This will tend to make you hook the ball to the left (Photo 24). The whole swing should therefore be aimed to the right of target. Again remember that it is likely to land on

24 Standing below the ball, the shot hooks to the left. Notice the difference in distance from the ball between 23 and 24.

25 Hitting downhill, the weight is kept well on the left foot, ball opposite the right foot. The ball will fly much lower than usual.

sloping ground so make sufficient allowance for this.

The way to remember which way the ball will bend is this – the ball will always curve in the air the same way it would roll on the ground. Standing above the ball it would roll to the right; it also curves to the right in flight. Standing below the ball it would roll to the left; it also curves to the left.

Hitting downhill

Hitting downhill – what is called a 'hanging lie' – is one of the most difficult shots of all. Firstly, it is difficult to strike the ball well. Secondly, the shot always flies much lower than normal. In other words, a 5-iron shot will fly like a 3-iron a 7-iron like a 5, and so on. This makes the long irons and woods very difficult.

In the stance, the ball must be positioned well back towards the right foot, with the weight very much on the left foot. This brings your shoulders in line with the slope so you can still take a proper swing (Photo 25). Take a club with plenty of loft – remembering that it will go a lot lower than usual – and try very hard in the swing to hit right *down* the slope. Never try to lift the ball. As you get a little experience with these shots, you will find that they curve slightly out to the right. Simply aim left to allow for this.

For the downhill shot, take a more lofted club than normal, play the ball more towards the right foot and aim left of target.

Hitting uphill

This is usually a fairly easy shot. The ball flies far higher than normal, making the long clubs especially easy. A 6-iron will travel like a normal 8-iron, the 4-iron like a 6-iron and so on. Play any short or medium iron as normal – keeping the weight on the left foot through the whole swing. For a longer shot with a long iron or wood you will have to make a real effort to push your weight onto the left foot as you strike the ball. The ball will usually curve away slightly to the left with these shots, so simply allow for this – aiming a little to the right of target.

49

11. Chipping

As you get closer to the green, you will need to adapt your swing to produce smaller, controlled shots. The first of these shots to learn is the chip. This is a little low shot, played with one of the medium irons – the 5, 6 or 7. The ball should skip a couple of yards through the air and then run the rest of the way to the hole (Action Sequence E).

The address position

You can use any of the medium irons for chipping – the 7-iron being the one we would suggest if you have a choice. But the 5 or 6 are really just as good. The main thing is to practise with one club and to feel confident with it. As you only want a small shot, hold further down the club and stand much closer to the ball, bending the knees rather more than for the long shots. Turn your feet slightly towards the target, feeling the weight is very much on the left foot. At this stage, have the hands well ahead of the ball and clubhead – to your left – with the left hand feeling very, very firm and the wrist really in control (Photo 26).

The swing

The main points about the chipping action are that the backswing and

50

throughswing should be exactly the same length, and the left hand and arm should do most of the work. Simply swing the club back eighteen inches or so with the left arm in control and let the knees turn a little to the right. Don't actually rock onto the right foot, the weight should stay on the left. Just turn the knees (Photo 27).

As you swing through, push the weight well onto your left foot, your right knee pointing through to the target. Try to keep the left wrist nice and firm as you strike the ball. Think very much about the position of your throughswing with the chip – keep the left arm perfectly straight and stop the club exactly the same length as your backswing (Photo 28). In this basic shot the club goes back eighteen inches and through eighteen inches. If you want a longer chip, you simply swing the club further back and through – again, the same swing either side. If you want a shorter shot, you take a shorter swing.

The common fault in chipping

Most golfers have one fault in chipping. They take the club too far back and then slow down as they hit the ball. When a player does this, the left arm stops moving just before hitting the ball and the left wrist folds up (Photo 29). This is quite wrong. The ball will then either run much too far along the ground, or

51

26

27

26/27/28 The basic chipping action.
The left wrist is kept very firm, head
absolutely still.

52

INCORRECT

29 Incorrect. The left hand has stopped moving before impact so that the left wrist has crumpled.

28
29

the clubhead will dig into the ground. Therefore, in chipping, always be quite certain that backswing and through-swing are exactly the same length – never letting the left wrist fold up. Lastly, keep the head perfectly still and only look up once the ball is well on its way to your target.

12. Pitching

The short pitch

This is the shot to use when there is a bunker or bank to go over. If there isn't anything in the way, the running chip shot with a medium iron is far safer. When you do have to pitch the ball up and over something, use the most lofted club you have – the highest number – or the sand wedge if you have one. With this, the ball will be lofted over the bunker but will land softly on the green the other side without running too far.

Again, as with the chip, go well down the grip of the club, stand in close to the ball, turn your feet a little towards your target and tighten your left hand so that the wrists are firm. Your hands should be slightly ahead of the ball, but not quite as far as with the chip (Photo 30).

Now swing the arms back, weight being kept towards the left foot, even though the legs may turn or rock a little (Photo 31). Then push the weight through onto your left foot and swing your arms with the same wooden action as for the chip, keeping your left wrist from bending (Photo 32).

Judging the distance

When you play a short pitch like this, always choose a definite spot where you want the ball to land. Having chosen

55

30

31

32

56

this spot, have two or three practice swings and make certain that the clubhead scrapes the ground as it goes through. If there is lots of grass, this is quite easy and one simply brushes the grass. If the ground is bare, make certain that the bottom of the club really does touch the ground lightly on each practice swing. With the ball, concentrate on exactly the same thing – brushing the ground. Picture the spot where you want the ball to land, but try to keep your head still for as long as you can after hitting the ball. You aren't likely to lose a ball from this distance, so there is no need to look up too quickly to see where it is going! As with chipping, a shorter swing will give a shorter shot and a longer swing will give a longer shot. However, it is very important to keep both halves of the swing the same length on every shot.

The long pitch

When you are playing a shot which is slightly shorter than your full shot with a 9-iron, it is played in a different way. For this shot one can use the 9-iron, 10-iron or sand wedge. This is very much like a full iron shot, except that the feet can be slightly narrower and

30/31/32 A short pitch over a bunker with a sand wedge. The club must scrape the ground as the ball is struck. This produces lots of height.

57

33 A long pitch shot with a wedge. The wrists cock early and freely.

34 At the end of a long pitch both arms are absolutely firm, punching the ball to the target.

turned a little towards the target. The ball is played opposite the centre of the stance, hands slightly to the left of the ball. In this shot, use plenty of wrist action in the backswing – feel that the swing is just to shoulder height (Photo 33). Now push the weight well onto the left foot and concentrate on hitting *down* through the ball, taking a divot. The difference between this shot and a full shot is in the finish. In the follow-through for the pitch shot, try to hit firmly but stop with a short, firm finish. Ideally, if you are strong enough, punch the ball away and finish with both arms straight and firm at around waist-height – the club pointing right out towards the target (Photo 34). As with all the other short shots, make quite certain that your head is perfectly still and keep looking down at the ground until after the ball has gone (Action sequence F).

13. Putting

Most juniors find putting very easy. There are really no set rules on the grip, stance and swing with putting. It is mainly a question of confidence and having a good eye for a ball. However, there are a few tips which might help you become a really good putter. Putting, like chipping, can improve your scores on the course most quickly.

The grip

Your ordinary golf grip is quite all right for putting but do make certain that your hands are well to the sides of the club, not with your right hand too far underneath. However, when you look at most professionals, you will see that they use a slightly different grip for putting. This is the reverse overlap grip. In this grip, the left first finger is the one which is on the outside and so keeps the two hands together, not the little finger of the right hand as is usually the case (Photo 35). This positioning of the left hand will often help you to push the putter straight back in the right direction and may give you a better stroke.

The putting stance

In putting, you can either crouch over the ball or stand up straight. Do

35 Jerry Pate. This shows the reverse overlap grip used in putting. His head is kept perfectly still until the ball drops in – most important.

whichever feels the more comfortable. There are three important things to remember in the stance:

1 Make certain that the putter sits flat on the ground. If either the heel or toe is off the ground, it makes it harder to roll the ball straight (Photo 36).

2 Check that your eyes are directly over the ball or very slightly inside it – in other words a little closer to your feet. This will help you judge the straight line to the hole. If your eyes are much too far over the ball, you will

61

36   The putting stance.

probably begin to pull the ball to the left.

3   Always keep your hands level with the ball, or slightly in front of it – *never behind it*.

The putting stroke

In a good putting stroke, the putter should move back and through smoothly, with the putter very low to the ground. Probably the most important thing about the putting stroke is to take a fairly short backswing so that you can push the club firmly at the hole. Never take a long backswing with a putt so that you have to slow down. Short back; firm through.

The other very important point about the putting stroke is to keep your head absolutely still. This will help you make the club travel in a perfectly straight line. If you move your head, you will usually find the putter travels off its line in the throughswing and is pulled in towards your feet. When you practise putting, and when you play, *never* look at the ball as it reaches the hole. With any putt of less than twelve feet, always keep your head perfectly still until you hear the ball drop in. Only look up once you hear it drop, or once you're sure it's missed!

Reading the greens

Once you have learnt a good putting stroke, you will need to be able to read the greens – judging the slope and aiming a little to one side or the other to allow for this. To do this, crouch down behind the ball and try to get a picture of the ground around the hole.

63

Once you have decided to allow a little to one side or the other, choose a spot to that side of the hole – as much as you think necessary – and then set-up and putt at this spot. Try to forget about the hole and just think of rolling the ball at the spot you have chosen. Deciding how hard to hit the ball is very much a question of practice and judgement – looking at the slope up or down to the hole.

Having chosen the line of the putt and decided how hard to strike it, remember the most important rule of all in putting – that of keeping the head perfectly still and listening for the ball to drop.

Practising putting – the stroke

Almost every golf club has a putting green to practise on. If you can learn to become a really good putter, this is where your scoring will improve most quickly. One of the best ways to learn a good putting stroke is to practise swinging the putter back and through between two other clubs. Lay two clubs down to make a kind of track, just a little wider than your putter head. Now simply practise swinging the club back and through, keeping it perfectly on line without touching the other two clubs (Photo 37).

Another good way of checking your putting stroke is by painting a circle, about quarter of an inch wide, right

37 Practising the putting stroke. Using a striped ball will also show you if you are rolling it correctly.

round the middle of the ball. Line up the ball so that this stripe aims at the hole (Photo 37). If you have a good putting stroke and roll the ball well, you will see that the stripe rolls over and over to the hole. If not, the ball will turn over to one side or the other.

65

Putting exercises

To practise short putts – eight feet or less – put six balls round the hole, all the same distance away. Just move round from one to the other, trying to hole all six. As soon as you miss one, pick the other balls out of the hole and start all over again until you can go right round the whole circle of six. This is fairly easy from three to four feet but not so easy from seven or eight feet!

A similar idea is to line up six balls in a row, the closest eighteen inches from the hole and the furthest about nine feet. Start with the closest first and then move back. Again, as soon as you miss one, pick all the balls out and start all over again. The advantage of both these exercises is that they make you try hard – just as you would on the course. They also give you a chance to see if your putting is improving steadily.

14. Bunker Shots

Bunker shots can be very, very easy. But you do need the right type of club. Most juniors unfortunately have to start playing without a sand wedge and this makes things unnecessarily difficult. The sand wedge is a very important club. As soon as you are old enough to use full size clubs, buy a really good sand wedge. Your professional will advise you. You will be able to use the club for many, many years, because it doesn't have to match the rest of your set of clubs. Many professionals use sand wedges which are twenty or thirty years old although they change the rest of their clubs every two or three years. But if you do have to start by playing the bunker shots with a 9-iron or 10-iron, the swing is just the same as with the sand wedge. You will just find it a little more difficult.

The splash shot

To play a ball from a bunker round the green, the basic idea is to aim at splashing out a circle of sand and the ball will pop out with it. To learn bunker shots in the practice bunker, draw a circle round the ball, from about three inches behind the ball to three inches in front of it. As you address the ball in a bunker shot, you are not allowed to touch the

sand, so you have to start by holding the clubhead half an inch or so above the sand. Start with the club just behind the back of the circle and *not* right by the ball. Now, the most important thing. *Don't* look at the ball but look at a spot in the sand at the back of the circle. At this stage, hold the clubface a little 'open' – in other words, with the face turned slightly to the right so that the club looks more lofted than normal. The ball is positioned well forwards toward the left foot (Photo 38).

The swing

Keep looking at the spot in the sand behind the ball and take a full, very slow swing, just splashing away the circle of sand. If you can splash out the sand, the ball will pop out too. Try very hard in this shot to stay looking down at the sand and not to look up too quickly to see where the ball has gone. Follow right through keeping your head very still (Action Sequence G).

Once you can do this by drawing a circle in the sand, try it by just choosing a spot in the sand, looking at this and imagining the circle of sand you are going to splash out.

Rules for good bunker shots

1   Look at a spot in the sand about three inches behind the ball and imagine the circle of sand to be splashed out.

38 Addressing the ball for the bunker splash shot. The clubface lies open, two or three inches behind the ball and above the sand. The eyes look at the sand behind the ball.

2 Take a full, slow swing and make sure you follow through. Don't chop at the ball too fast or the club will stick in the sand.

3 If you want a slightly longer shot, think of a smaller circle of sand round the ball – looking one and a half or two inches behind the ball. If you want a shorter shot, look four inches behind the ball and splash out more sand.

4 If you open the face of the club with your bunker shots (Photo 38), then you may find that the ball pops out to the

39 With a buried ball, the clubface is square, not open. This shot requires strength and confidence.

right of target every time. Simply choose an imaginary target six or eight feet to the left of the flag and aim at this. Now the ball should splash out towards the flag (Action sequence H).

The buried ball

If your ball buries itself in the sand, the shot is played entirely differently. This time, the clubhead is never opened to increase the loft but held in the normal, square position. Push the hands a little further to the left than usual and look at a spot in the sand just behind the ball.

Now lift the club quite high in the back-swing, push the weight firmly onto the left foot swing down and really smash through the sand and ball. This shot is just strength and confidence (Photo 39).

The long bunker shot

If you need a long shot from a bunker, firstly look at the shot from the side to see how much height you need to get over the bank in front. Never make the mistake of choosing a club which won't get enough height. If the ball is sitting right up on top of the sand, try to pick it off completely cleanly without touching the sand at all. Look at the back of the ball just as you would with a normal iron shot. If you tend to take too much sand with this shot you can even try looking at the top of the ball.

If the ball is sitting down in the sand, play the shot just like an iron shot with a divot. Hit *down* and through the ball and then the sand and this will force it out. From any lie like this don't be too ambitious with the club you choose. It is much better to come out safely with a good 9-iron shot than play a poor 7-iron and hit the bank in front.

Finally, smooth over your footprints as you leave the sand – very important.

A word for parents

Bunker shots are usually rather un-natural even for the most talented

young junior. If they once learn them the wrong way it is often hard to undo this and teach the correct method. Therefore always see that your junior has professional coaching on this shot in particular. Points to stress are the slowness and fullness of the swing, looking at the sand and *not* the ball and following through with the weight on the left foot. Lastly, this is the part of the game where the right equipment is essential. The sooner your junior can be given a sand wedge the better his chances of learning to play the correct type of shot.

15. Learning from Others

As a junior golfer you can learn a great deal from watching good golfers. If you are lucky enough to be able to go to professional tournaments, spend plenty of time watching the best players practising. You can learn an awful lot from this. Let's take a look at the type of things you will see in every good golfer's swing and the important points to copy.

Address

Most important here is the grip. You will see just about every good golfer with the right hand nicely *behind* the club, all the strength in it aimed down the fairway to the flag. You will also see the weight towards the insides of the feet with the knees knocked in a little. The professional will probably play the ball further towards the left foot than you can at present, but notice how straight the left arm is and how the right one is a little bent. This you can copy (Photo 40). If you look down the practice ground from behind, you will always see feet, knees, hips and shoulders aimed straight down the line of the shot. Remember the 'railway lines' – ball along the right one, body down the left.

40   Jack Nicklaus at address. Think of those 'railway lines' he is aiming along – body along the left one, ball along the right. Notice the right hand very much behind the club.

41   *Facing page*: Tom Weiskopf. The takeaway is smooth with the hands already beginning to work.

Takeaway

Watch how the good golfer takes the club away very smoothly – not with a quick jerk. Watch the left arm, shoulder and knee and you will see that they are doing most of the work. The hands will probably not seem to be doing much, but if you look at them very closely, you will see that they really begin to move

right from the moment the club starts back (Photo 41).

Backswing

If you look at this position from behind, you will see that the left arm has come right across towards the right shoulder, so that the elbows seem nice and close. The back is fully turned to the target but the professional is doing all this turn by thinking of the left side and left shoulder, not the right. Of course this happens very quickly, but you will never see a professional with a loose grip at this point. It is always really firm, with the left hand well in control

75

of the club. Lastly, something a little more advanced. The club at the top will be pointing in the direction of the shot – down the left railway line. But notice the angle of the clubhead and wrist. From a good grip – and remember this – the back of the left wrist should be very nearly straight with the clubhead pointing down the line of the arm. This type of position is known as a 'square position', because it is the easiest for bringing the clubface into the square position – the one where it looks at the target – in the downswing. Once you become a good golfer, this very firm, solid position at the top is something to work on with professional advice (Photo 42).

Downswing

The movement in this part of the swing is, of course, very fast. But you can learn a lot from this photo if not from watching the swing itself (Photo 43). What you will see is the tremendous pull of the left hand and arm. From the top of the backswing, the right arm and right shoulder mustn't do too much; it is the left you have to think of. The left arm pulls down to start the downswing, the left heel pushed firmly back to the ground, so that the wrists are still cocked or bent as they were at the top of the swing. Work hard with the

76

42 Lou Graham. A perfect backswing.
Look at the straight left arm and position
of the right. A key for advanced players —
the line along the clubface points down the
line of the left arm.

left hand and arm and you will soon get
this perfect action.

Impact

This is the most important part of the
swing. You will see lots of differences in
the good players' swings, but they are
all in much the same position here

77

43 Donna Young – twice American Open Champion. The left heel is firmly back on the ground, with the left arm and hand pulling hard down to impact.

(Photo 44). The first thing to notice is the head; the eyes are really looking at the ball – not looking up the fairway as yours might be! Next look at the left arm. Again the power and speed in that is obvious, it is working very hard and fast. The right arm, on the other hand, isn't quite straight yet. Lastly, the left heel. The good golfer pushes the weight

78

44 Jo Anne Carner. A perfect impact position from one of the world's longest hitting women golfers, and former American Champion.

back onto the left heel in the downswing so that he is firmly on this as the ball is struck. In fact, you will often see the toes off the ground, but the heel is right down (Photo 45).

Beyond the ball

Here again, the emphasis is on the left side. Pushing the left heel down to the

45 Gary Player at impact with an iron. The left leg is now firm, right foot spinning through onto the toes. The eyes are still looking down where the ball was.

ground means that the left leg will be really firm (Photo 46). People often talk of 'hitting against the left leg' and this is what they mean. Look, too, at the left arm. The good golfer's left arm always turns so that it folds *into* the body, elbow down. The club golfer's arm usually crumples outwards instead. The left arm should be very much in control.

80

46   Johnny Miller. Notice the firm left leg and position of the right foot. The left arm is folding into the body, grip firm.

Now look at the right leg. The knee is just beginning to point on through to the target, so it has worked smoothly through impact. Don't be left back on the right foot at this stage. Lastly, and perhaps most important, the eyes are still looking down at the spot where the ball was, even though it is well on its way. If you imitate this, more than any-

47　Severiano Ballesteros. A perfect, full followthrough.

thing else, you will soon find yourself striking the ball better and more consistently. Remember, however, that you can stay down too long, which may restrict the followthrough.

The finish

The finish of the swing nearly always shows how good the swing has been. It is a real check for you. The professional golfer almost always holds a good finish for a couple of seconds; the club golfer never even gets a followthrough on most shots! So, copy the professional and make certain you really do swing to a full finish (Photo 47).

The first thing to look at here is the leg position. The left heel is flat on the ground, toes often upwards, the left leg is usually quite straight and firm and the right knee points to the target, the right foot balanced on the tips of the toes. This means that the hips and shoulders are turned through to face the flag. At this stage, both arms are bent and the club is back over the shoulder. Another point for you to imitate is the grip – still perfectly firm and in control. So, left heel down, right knee through and a very firm grip.

83

16. Becoming a Champion

No one becomes a champion at any sport without lots and lots of hard work and practice. Some, of course, practise harder than others, but all great golfers have had to work hard at their game at some stage in their lives. The younger you are when you do all this hard work, the sooner you are likely to become a champion (Photo 48).

Getting the most from your practice

If you want to become a champion, then you will need to practise hard and long hours. The better you plan your practice the more benefit it will be. Many players set themselves a schedule of practice and stick to this each day. Others keep a notebook of the amount they practise and the types of shots they have hit. If you practise with a plan in mind you will find you improve much more quickly. You could plan your practice as follows: twenty 9-irons, twenty 7-irons, twenty 5-irons, twenty 3-irons and twenty drives. If you are a hard worker, you might make this up to 100 of each by your mid-teens. It really depends on just how good you want to be and how determined you are to succeed. You will also need to practise putting, chipping and pitching and

48 Severiano Ballesteros enjoying being interviewed by press and television after one of his championship wins. But don't forget all the hard work the public doesn't see.

bunker shots – all of which take time to learn to play well. The amount you can do will depend very much on the facilities that are available. But even practising chipping in the garden – if allowed – will train you to control the ball well and to become a better player (Photo 49).

Charting your progress

Once you begin to play in junior championships, you may find it helpful to know exactly where you are going

49 A makeshift practice exercise – pitching into an umbrella.

wrong on the course. Many professionals keep an exact record of the number of putts they take on every round, whether they are short with their shot to the green or whether they hit the ball too far; whether they miss the green or the fairway to the right or left. If you think back over your round of golf afterwards and keep a record of this, you may find, for example, that you tend to take too little club to the green very often – or that you are taking too many putts. This can then be helpful in knowing what to practise.

Learning a new course

One of the things which is likely to be difficult when you first go to play in junior championships, is learning to play a new course. On your own course you will know from experience which club to take for each shot. On a different course, you may well find it difficult to judge the distances. If you don't take the right club to the green, you will lose shots. If you watch almost all professional golfers playing in tournaments, you will see that they keep a notebook of the distances on the course, having paced these out on the practice round the day before. If you want to become a champion, this is something to learn.

The idea is to choose a bunker or tree somewhere near where you expect to drive. Make a note of which bunker you have chosen – whether on the left or right – and pace the distance from this tree or bunker to the centre or front of the green as you prefer. Take fairly large steps and these – for most teenagers – should be roughly a yard. Make a note of the distance. The next day, pace from the spot you have marked to your ball and you can simply work out the distance to the green. To make really good use of this, you will need to know exactly how far you hit the ball with each club. Do this by hitting balls on the practice ground and stepping off the distances for each club. Once you learn to do this, you will find it quite simple to learn a new course very quickly.

The tournament professional usually measures off the length of the green and sends his caddie out each morning to find out where each flag is. So he really knows on every shot the distance from his ball to the flag to within a yard or so. If the wind is against, he will take one club longer; if the wind is behind, he will take one club shorter. But he really works very hard preparing for a tournament.

Ideas to help you

If you are not able to have a practice round, here are some ideas to help you judge a new course.

1 A very flat course is often misleading. There is usually a lot of 'dead ground' – ground you don't see because of the flatness – which makes the distance seem shorter than it is. Always take a longer club than you think necessary.

2 Try to judge the distance to the green when the people in front are on it. The reason for this is simple. Flags on various greens are not always the same size. A very short flag will often look much further away than it is and a very tall flag will seem much nearer. The people in front give you something constant by which to judge distance. You may also find it difficult to judge distances with very tall trees behind the

green. Again, this trick of sizing up against the people in front is helpful.

3 Never think what club you are going to take until you reach the ball. If you start judging the distance before you get there, you may keep changing your mind and that never helps.

4 Watch out for any bunker which appears to be in front of a green. Often there is 15 or 20 yards of dead ground behind it which you won't see and this may make you underclub and drop short. Again, if you see the people in front walking to the green this may give you an idea of the distance. Count the number of steps they take – roughly a yard each – between bunker and green.

5 Always think carefully about the wind if any. Most golfers, even pros, find it difficult to judge the clubbing into the wind. Really make sure you take enough club. You are most unlikely to go through the green. Beware of a tee which is sheltered by trees. Where your ball is going to be landing, on the fairway or green, the wind may be very strong. Try to think of this and allow for the wind although you cannot feel it. Look at the way the flag is flapping, to help judge the wind.

6 Whenever you are walking past another fairway or green of a hole you haven't played, look at it. Learn what you can about the layout of the hole and position of the flag.

89

7   Bear in mind that on most holes the bunkers by the green are at the front. Do as most professionals do. Always take enough club and if you go off line you will usually find you miss most of the bunkers and only leave yourself a chip. Most amateur golfers are always short on every shot to the green. Take enough club and save shots.

Things to practise

One of the most important points for the good golfer is to strengthen the left hand and arm so that they can work just as hard as the right side. The more you can practise with the left arm, the stronger it will become. At first, simply start by swinging the club right back and through with your left arm only. Take a full backswing, making sure the arm is really straight, and then swing through so that the left arm forms a right angle – the elbow downwards (Photo 50). This is very important. Don't simply swing right through with the arm perfectly straight. This isn't what happens in the ordinary swing and so will only teach you bad habits. Make sure that the left arm moves into this kind of position – folding into the body as it should in the swing.

Once you can swing the club like this with the left arm only, try to learn to hit balls like this, with a 6 or 7-iron. This will help strengthen the arm a great deal

90

50 Strengthen the left arm with one-armed swings, but always let the arm bend correctly in the followthrough.

and make it work as hard and fast as the right. It is also helpful to practise both chipping and putting with the left arm only, thus learning control and strengthening the left hand and wrist.

Training exercises

Physical training is important in golf – particularly to strengthen the legs and arms. One of the best leg exercises is to stand with one foot up on a firm chair. Then push yourself up very slowly onto this leg so that you are standing on one leg on the chair. Lower yourself down again very slowly – the slower the better. Then push back up again and down again. Repeat this twenty times on each leg, pushing up and down as slowly as possible. This will strengthen the legs enormously.

To strengthen the arms and wrists, one of the best exercises is to tie a weight – a brick for example – onto a piece of strong stick, with a yard or so of string. Hold the stick in both hands, at arms length, with the weight dangling loosely. Then, keeping the arms straight, roll the stick over and over in your hands to wind up the string and pull the weight upwards. You will find this very hard work at first. Once it becomes easy, use a heavier weight so that the muscles are always kept working hard.

As a last reminder, if you want to become a champion golfer or if you are

51 Some of the superstars practising for the British Open – often for many hours each day.

ever thinking of becoming a professional, remember that it requires hard work. The life of a champion golfer looks very glamorous to people watching, but don't forget all the hours of practice he or she has put in to reach that standard (Photo 51).

93

17. Equipment

Anyone beginning to play golf – whether as a junior or an adult – doesn't need to begin with a full set of fourteen clubs like the professional. It is far better to start with a few clubs and to learn to use each of these well (Photos 52 & 53).

The putter

This is the club designed for use on the green or around the green, when the ball is simply rolled – putted – along the ground. The putter is generally a short club, often with a completely different shaped head from the rest of the clubs.

52 The full range of clubs.

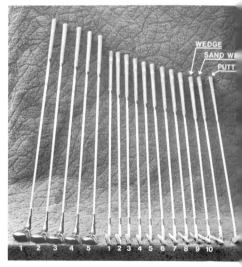

Because the putter is simply designed to roll the ball along the ground, the face of the club – the part which hits the ball – has hardly any angle of loft. However, in buying a putter, avoid one with no loft at all as this will only work on greens in tip-top tournament condition.

The irons

When we look at the iron clubs, these are graded in lofts – in other words, in the angle of the club faces – to give a range of different height shots. At the lowest end we have the 1-iron which has very little loft and so produces a very low shot, and at the other end, the 10-iron which has the face set at a con-

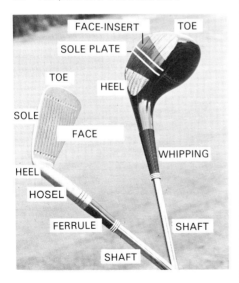

53 The parts of a wood and iron.

FACE-INSERT TOE
SOLE PLATE
TOE
HEEL
SOLE
FACE
WHIPPING
HEEL
HOSEL
FERRULE SHAFT
SHAFT

siderable angle to produce a high shot. All the other clubs are graded in between. As well as having this difference in loft, the lengths of the clubs are graded so that the 3-iron is half an inch longer than the 4-iron, the 4-iron is half an inch longer than the 5 and so on. This helps produce a range of different heights and lengths of shots – the higher the number, the shorter the shot.

There is no set distance which each club will hit the ball. The important thing is that they produce a full range of distances. A professional might expect to hit the ball 190 yards with a 3-iron, 160 yards with a 6-iron and 130 yards with a 9-iron. A good woman golfer might expect to hit 170 yards with the 3-iron, 140 yards with the 6-iron and 110 yards with the 9-iron. The distances are going to be much less for the young player but the clubs will still make a noticeable difference in the length and height of shots they produce.

Lastly, in the set of irons, is the sand wedge – a club with the equivalent of 11-iron loft. This is the most lofted club of all, designed for playing the ball out of sand bunkers and for various other shots around the green.

The woods

The woods are numbered in a similar way to the irons – this time from 1 to 5. Again, the face of the club has more loft

96

the higher the number. The difference in the length of the clubs is also the same as for the irons – the 3-wood being half an inch longer than the 4 and so on. Because these are the clubs used to produce the longest shots of all, they are several inches longer than the irons to provide extra power.

The 1 and 2-woods are mainly used for driving – the first shot on the hole where the ball is teed up on a tee-peg to help produce maximum distance. For this reason the 1-wood is always called the driver – the 2-wood being used as an alternative to this for the golfer who isn't an expert. The 3, 4 and 5-woods are known as the fairway woods because they are mainly used from the fairway – the cut part of the course between the tee and the green. As with the irons, the 3 produces a lower, longer shot than the 4, and the 5-wood produces a higher and shorter shot than the 4. A professional might expect to hit the 3-wood 220 yards and the 5-wood 200 yards, while the good woman player would expect, perhaps, 190 yards from the 3-wood and 170 yards from the 5-wood.

Choosing your clubs

The main point in choosing your clubs or having them altered to suit you is to make sure that they are the right weight and length. Never use a golf club which is too heavy. Adults often think that if

97

they give a junior heavy clubs, he or she will become strong using them. This is quite wrong. You won't be able to swing a heavy club well and will soon develop a poor swing. Many great golfers use surprisingly light clubs. Jack Nicklaus, for example, uses clubs which are probably quite a bit lighter than the clubs used by many average players. In fact, golf club makers are always experimenting to make lighter golf shafts and clubs because they are easier to use.

For under 12's

If you are starting as a really young junior, all you need is a few clubs cut down to size – a wood, 2 or 3 irons and a putter. Probably you will have to rely on what your parents or professional can find to suit you. The ideal wood is probably a 3 or 4; this can be used for both driving from the tee and for playing the fairway shots. As for the irons, the ideal would be one of the long irons (the 3 or 4), a medium iron (the 5, 6 or 7) and then one of the short irons (the 8 to sand wedge). Ideally, I suppose, a 4-iron, 7-iron and wedge would be the best choice. The main thing is that you have a variety of clubs to play different length shots. Lastly, of course, you will need a putter.

Make sure these clubs are cut down to the right size. Having clubs which are too long is just as bad as having clubs which are too heavy; they won't help you to develop a good swing. The professional at your local club will be able to cut these down and re-grip them. The wood will need to be about three inches above your waist, the longest of the irons about four inches shorter than this with a half inch between each number, and the putter about two inches shorter than your shortest iron.

It is very important for the young junior to have thin enough grips on the club. If the grips are thin you will be able to grip the club correctly; if they are too thick you won't be able to learn the correct grip. Ask your professional to re-grip them to suit your hands – ideally with a thin leather grip.

Lastly, if you are starting with old clubs cut down to size, these may be the kind with brown shafts, rather than silver coloured, chromium-plated shafts. If so, you may find the numbers on each iron are a little different from newer clubs. Ask your professional or a golfing friend to tell you the equivalent in the newer numbering as this will help you follow the instructions in this book or any other.

The over 12's

Most boys over the age of 12 will be able to use ordinary ladies' clubs, moving on to use men's clubs in their middle teens according to size and strength.

54 Gary Player and his caddie lining up a most important putt.

Again, don't be in too much of a hurry to use heavy clubs; keep swinging a club which you can control really well rather than using heavy clubs which begin to swing you! Girls will probably need to use cut-down clubs until they are about thirteen or so – depending very much on individual height and strength. Certainly you don't want to be using full size ladies' clubs until you are at least five feet tall. Up until that time a slightly cut down club or junior model is the ideal thing.

For this age group, the ideal is a half set – in other words a 2 or 4-wood (or driver and 4-wood) and the 3, 5, 7, 9 and sand wedge, plus a putter. If these are being bought new for you, (or you are buying them yourself), ask your professional to choose a make which you will be able to add to. Many club makers change their designs every year; others keep their models available longer and this gives you a chance to build up your set.

Once you begin to play in tournaments in your mid-teens you will probably find you want a full set of clubs. At this stage you will begin to find too much difference in the length of shots between the 3, 5, 7 and 9-irons and so feel you need all the irons. At this stage you will probably want all the irons from 3 to sand wedge – the 1- and 2-iron only being clubs for real experts. As for the woods, this is very much a personal choice. A 1, 3 and 4 is a common selection amongst men and 1, 3 and 5 or 1, 3, 4 and 5 amongst women.

A word for parents

1 Clubs which are too long and heavy won't strengthen your junior's swing. They will ruin it.

2 Ensure that the grips really are thin enough – a layer of tape or thin leather grip being essential for a young junior.

3 If you are buying any new clubs make sure you choose a make and model which you can add to in the future.

18. Par and Handicapping

Many years ago when golf was first played, golf courses varied greatly in length. They were simply built on common land, usually beside the sea, and the number of holes varied with the area of the land. Some had as few as five holes – others as many as twenty-five. However, the most famous of the old courses, St Andrews, had eighteen holes and the rest of the world eventually copied what happened at St Andrews. Almost all courses therefore have eighteen holes – or in some cases nine holes, in which case one usually plays round twice.

Par for the course

The idea of golf, as you probably know, is to complete each hole in as few shots as possible. But as the holes vary in length, the player is likely to need more shots for the longer ones and less for the shorter ones. Holes are therefore rated for length and difficulty. This we call the par. For men, a par-3 is anything from 100 yards to 250 yards. This means that a good golfer should be able to hit the green with one long shot and he is then supposed to have two putts – a total of 3. So this is a par-3.

From 251 yards to 475 yards he would be expected to reach the green with two long shots plus his two putts – giving a total of four. So these we call par-4's. Anything over 476 yards we would expect to take him three long shots, plus his two putts, giving us the par-5's. When we add the pars for the eighteen holes, we have the par for the course, usually something between 66 and 74, and this is the measure of length and difficulty of the course. This is the number of strokes the really good player would expect to take to complete the course.

For ladies, most of the holes are rather shorter than for men – the ladies play off tees in front of the men's. For this reason, the par for ladies is slightly different – a par-3 being up to about 220 yards, a par-4 from 220 to around 400 yards and a par-5 anything over 400 yards. For most of you as juniors, whether boys or girls, you will first be playing from the ladies' tees to make the course slightly shorter and easier – the boys moving back to the men's tees as their standard improves.

Basic handicapping

Having got the par of the course, this gives us a way of comparing standards of players. The good golfer would hope to go round the course in approximately par figures. Let's say we have a

course with a par of 72. If a player usually goes round in about 75 then we would say that his handicap is (75–72), that is 3. A player who isn't quite so good, might usually take 87 to go round so that his handicap would be (87–72), that is 15 and so on. The very best players expect to go round in par, 72, so that their handicap is zero – what we call scratch. If they are even better than this, then their handicaps may become plus 1 or plus 2, meaning that they are expected to go round the course in less than par. Players with handicaps like this are usually international team players.

The maximum handicap a man can have is 24 – even if his scores are over 100 and so would give him a higher handicap than this. On the other hand, ladies can have handicaps up to 36. Most of you as juniors will be allowed to start with handicaps up to 36 and probably, if you start very young, up to 54. In some clubs, young juniors are handicapped on 9-holes or even given special tees ahead of the ladies' tees. So there is a certain amount of variation from one club to another.

What a handicap does mean, however, is that golfers of all standards can compete against each other and everyone has a reasonable chance of winning.

19. Scoring in Golf

Strokeplay

There are two basic ways of scoring. The first is called strokeplay. In this, you add the scores for the 18 holes, writing them down on the card provided. This total gives the gross score. From this you deduct your handicap to give the nett score. If you have a handicap of 36 and go round the course in 107, this gives a nett score of 71. Players then compare nett scores and the lowest score wins. Usually in this type of competition, a scratch prize is also given for the best gross score – so going to the best player in the competition regardless of handicap.

Matchplay

The other way of scoring is a direct match with one other person. In this you compare the scores on each hole and the player with the lower score wins the hole. To give both players an equal chance, handicap strokes are given. If, for example, you are 36 handicap and your opponent is 24, then you would receive three-quarters of the difference in handicap, in other words three-quarters of (36–24), which is 9. You are then said to be receiving 9 strokes. This means that on 9 holes of the course, you would subtract

Look at the very short, smooth backswing required for this 20-yard chip. The ball is played close to the feet, hands well down the club and the head really stays still long after the ball has gone

In the long pitch, the hands work early and freely in the backswing, but the ball is punched away to the target with the left arm staying absolutely straight and stretched in this short, firm followthrough

The swing in the bunker shot is full and very, very slow. The eyes are looking about 2 inches behind the ball and the aim is simply to splash out a circle of sand – the ball popping out too

In playing a bunker shot, the clubface is laid back so that it aims out to the right. This increases the height of the shot. The whole stance and swing is therefore aimed left to allow for this but the ball pops out on-target

one stroke from your score before comparing it with your opponent's score. To find out where you receive your 9 strokes, look on the scorecard for the column marked stroke index. You then receive a stroke on every hole with a number 9 or less against it. Your professional or junior organizer will always explain this to you when you first play.

Now on the first hole, let's imagine that you have a 6 and your opponent takes 5, but you have a stroke. This means that you have a nett score of 5, taking your stroke away, and when you compare this with your opponent's score, they are the same. This means that you halve the hole. If you take 7 and your opponent takes 6 and you don't get a stroke, then he would win the hole. If you both take 6 and you have a stroke, then you would win the hole.

Now supposing you win the first hole, then you become 1 up and your opponent would be 1 down. If you win the next hole, you become 2 up and so on. If the score is level, then we say the players are all square. In theory one could play all 18 holes and see which player was leading at the end. However, the match can often be won before all 18 holes are played. If, for example, you finish the 15th hole and are 4 up, there are only 3 holes left on the course for

106

your opponent to catch you. Therefore even if he won all the other 3 holes, you couldn't be beaten. So we say that you have won by '4 & 3'. Whenever you are more holes up than there are holes to be played, you would have won. Examples of match results are '5 & 4', meaning you were 5 holes up with only 4 left to play, '2 & 1', meaning that you were 2 up with only 1 left and so on. The most anyone can be beaten is '10 & 8', losing all the first 10 holes so that there are only 8 left!

One point of etiquette – in other words, politeness – is that the person who is losing in the match should state the score at the end of each hole. This saves any confusion about the score.

Stableford bogey

This is a popular alternative to the ordinary strokeplay competition. In this competition players are given seven-eighths of their handicap. These strokes are taken, rather like in matchplay, at the holes shown in the stroke index on the card – deducting the stroke when shown from the score for that hole. Points are then given in relation to par, as shown:

1 over par	1 point
par	2 points
1 under par (birdie)	3 points
2 under par (eagle)	4 points

Sequence E
A basic chipping action

Sequence F
Playing the long pitch with
a wedge

Sequence G
The bunker splash shot

Sequence H
A splash shot, showing the
direction of the stance and
swing

The points for each hole are added up –
the highest score wins.

Foursomes and fourballs

As well as being played as individuals,
golf can be played as partnerships. The
two basic forms of this are foursomes
and fourballs. In foursomes, the two
players play alternate shots with the
same ball. If player A drives on the 1st
hole, player B drives on the 2nd, player
A on the third and so on, taking
alternate shots on each hole. The
competition can then take the form of
match, strokeplay or stableford.

In a fourball, each player plays his
own ball. A and B act as partners, the
usual form of scoring is to take the
better of their two scores for each hole –
therefore it is simply known as the
'better ball'. This is a slow form of golf
and takes far longer than a single or
foursome, so that juniors playing a
fourball aren't likely to be popular!

Eclectic

Very often, your junior club will run an
eclectic competition. The idea of this is
to record the lowest score you do for
each hole during the period of the
competition. You may find that an
eclectic is run throughout the summer
holidays, in which case every time you
go out to play you can try to better
your score on any hole. Sometimes you

55 Tony Jacklin. Another perfect
backswing to copy.

will be limited to the number of cards
you can do – say six cards. But some
clubs allow you to do as many cards as
you like. Usually half the handicap is
deducted at the end of the competition.

These, then, are the basic forms of
competition. There are others but your
junior organizer will be ready to explain
these if they arise.

20. Etiquette

Most adult golfers are encouraging to up-and-coming junior players. However, you will only be treated well by your club members if you follow the etiquette – good manners – expected of all golfers. Follow these carefully. Some are concerned with safety, others with protecting the condition of the course and the rest are simply accepted as politeness.

1   When watching someone else play, always stand directly opposite him, in other words with the ball between the two of you. Never stand behind him; this can be both distracting and dangerous. Stand perfectly still and keep quiet.

2   Keep your bag and trolley away from the greens and off any tees and repair any damage you do to the course – pitch marks on the green or divots on the fairway. If you take a divot on the tee, the correct etiquette is not to replace it – this is the one time when you don't. Smooth over any footprints you make in bunkers.

3   If you play on your own you have no real standing on the course and you *must* let other players through. Otherwise, if playing in a two or threeball, always stand aside and wave the people behind through if you are holding them up. Most adults hate to be held up by juniors so let them through. Having waved them on, let them get well out of range before continuing.

4   Never hit into the people playing ahead of you. Obviously it is very difficult when you are learning and are not quite sure of the distance you can hit, but really do make sure they are out of range. If you are unfortunate enough to hit into them, apologize as soon as possible.

5   If you think there is any danger of your ball hitting someone, shout 'Fore'. If you hear someone shout 'Fore', don't look round to see if he means you. Cover your head with your arms, preferably bend over and hope if it does hit you it isn't on your head. (Incidentally, ask your parents to insure you against hitting anyone or being hit. Nasty accidents can happen.)

6   Never tread on the line of your opponent's putt, i.e. between his ball and the hole. Be very careful not to damage the green – never stand right by the edge of the hole, scuff the green with your spikes or run across it. If you take the flag out, place it on the green. Don't drop it.

7   If you are asked to attend the flag, loosen it first to make sure it will come out, hold the cloth part of the flag if you can reach it to stop it flapping and keep your shadow away from the hole or line of the putt. Pull the flag out *as soon as your opponent putts*.

8   If you have to mark your ball on the green to clean it or because it is in someone else's line, put a small coin or marker down right behind the ball and then pick up the ball. To replace it, put the ball down first, right where it was originally, and then pick up the marker.

9   Tell your partner or opponent on the first tee what kind of ball you are playing and tell him if you change it.

10   In a match state the score at the end of every hole if you are the player who is down.

Golfing Terms

Address – the position from which you prepare to hit the ball.

Airshot – missing the ball altogether.

All square – when the players are even in a match.

Birdie – a hole done in one less than the par (standard score).

Caddie – a person who carries a player's clubs and can advise him if asked.

Chip – a short shot from just off the edge of the green, played with a medium iron – 5, 6 or 7.

Divot – the piece of turf cut up in playing an iron shot.

Eagle – a hole completed in 2 less than the par (standard score).

Eclectic – a competition run over a period of several weeks, when players try to improve their score for each hole.

Face – the part of the club with which you hit the ball.

Fairway – the cut part of the course from the tee to the green.

Fore – the word to shout if you think your ball may hit anyone.

Fourball – a partnership game where each player plays a ball and the lower score of the partnership is counted.

Foursome – players play in pairs, but use one ball and hit alternate shots with it.

Gross score – the score before deducting a player's handicap.

Handicap – this is a measure of a player's standard, and is the number of strokes over par in which he should complete the course. Example; if the par is 72, a player with an 8 handicap would expect to go round in $(72 + 8) = 80$.

Honour – the player who has the lowest score on each hole plays first from the next tee – taking the honour.

Hook – a shot which bends from right to left in the air.

Medal – another name for strokeplay in which the strokes taken for every hole are added up.

Nett score – your score after deduction of handicap.

Par – the standard score a good player would expect to take for each hole. The total of these gives the par for the course.

Pull – a shot which flies straight left of target.

Push – a shot which goes straight right of target.

Scratch golfer – a player expected to go round in par.

Slice – a shot which bends severely from left to right.

Stroke index – the column on the card which tells you where to receive or give your handicap strokes.